For Eileen and Lin

First published in Great Britain in 1988 by Andersen Press Limited

Picturemac edition published 1990 by
MACMILLAN CHILDREN'S BOOKS
A division of Macmillan Publishers Limited
London and Basingstoke
Associated companies throughout the world

ISBN 0-333-51423-8

A CIP catalogue record for this book is available from the British Library

Printed in Singapore

ALPHABET

PUZZLE

?

~ Jill Downie ~

MACMILLAN CHILDREN'S BOOKS

A, a

is for

axe

bark

C, c

is for

camel

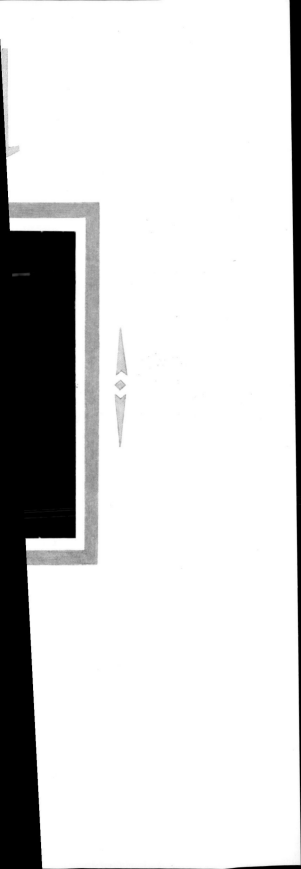

desert

E,e

is for

egg

frying-pan

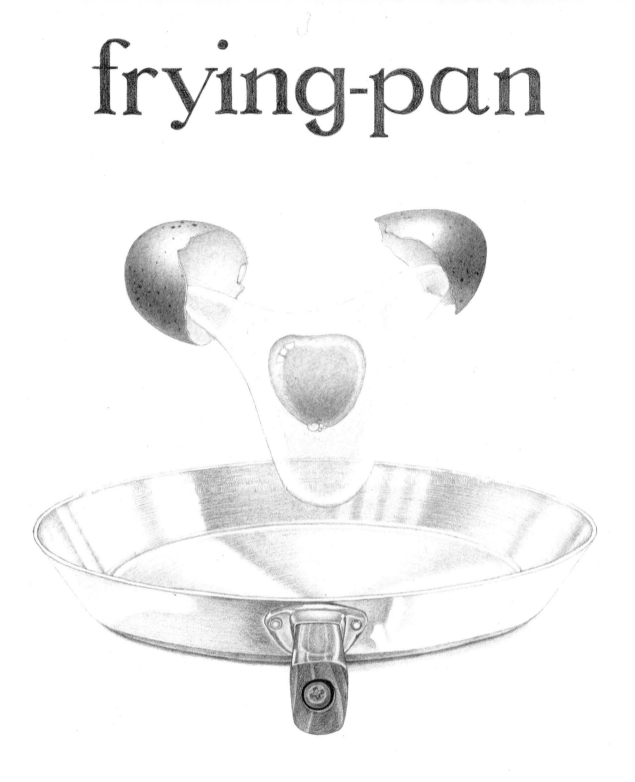

G,g

is for
garland

hat

I, i

is for
icicles

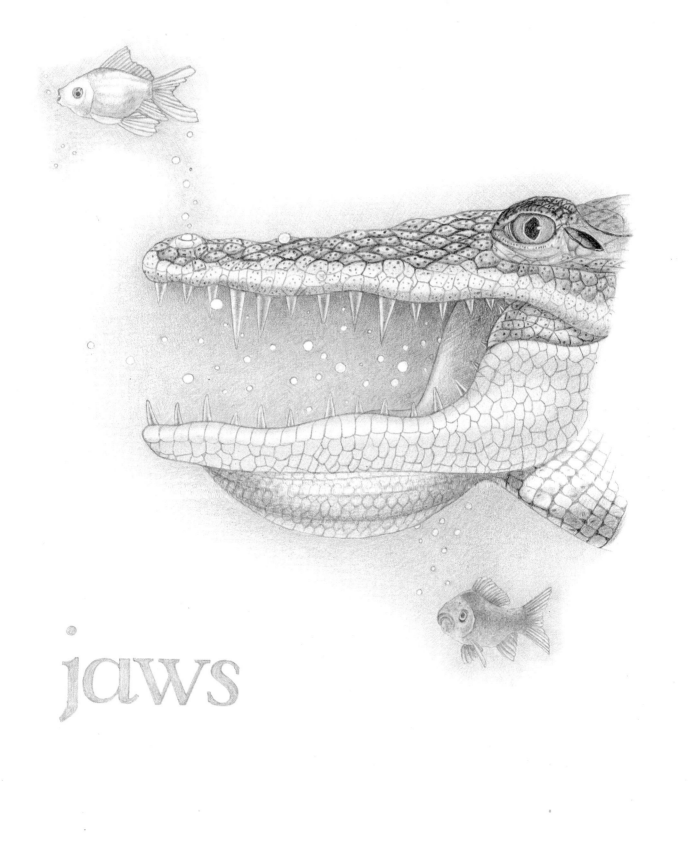

jaws

K,k

is for
kite

ladder

M,m

is for

moon

nightingale

O,o

is for

oven

picnic

Q q

is for

quiver

reeds

S,s

is for
shoes

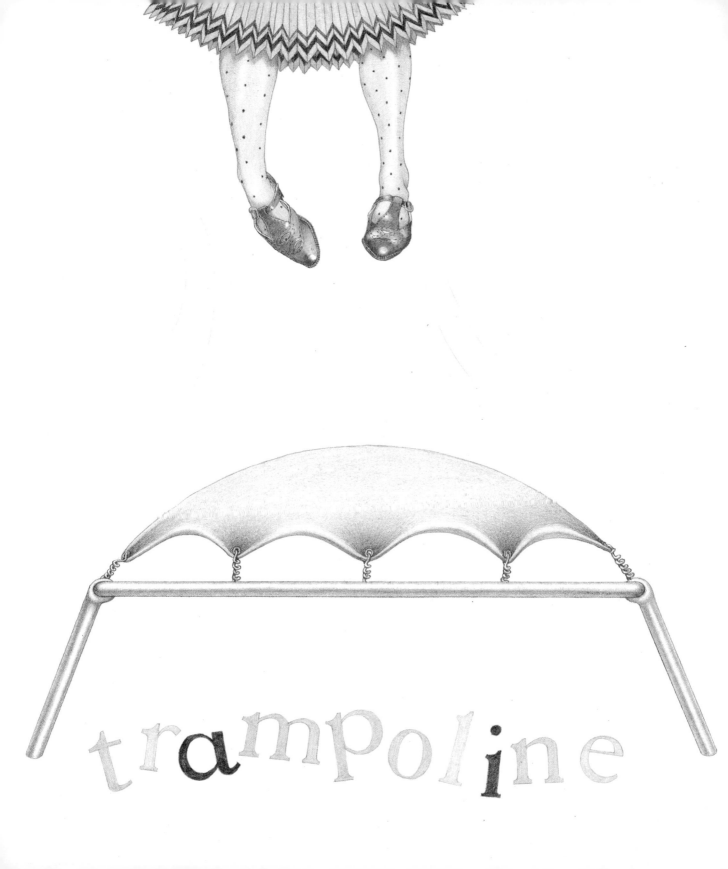

trampoline

U,u

is for
umbrella

vase

W,w

is for
waves

Y, y

is for
yak

zig-zag

Other Picturemacs you will enjoy

JACK AND NANCY Quentin Blake
A WALK IN THE PARK Anthony Browne
THROUGH THE MAGIC MIRROR Anthony Browne
I'LL TAKE YOU TO MRS COLE! Nigel Gray/Michael Foreman
MAYBE IT'S A TIGER Kathleen Hersom/Niki Daly
AARDVARK'S PICNIC Jon Atlas Higham
THE ADVENTURES OF ALBERT, THE RUNNING BEAR Barbara Isenberg/
  Susan Wolf/Dick Gackenbach
PINKERTON, BEHAVE! Steven Kellogg
THE MICE NEXT DOOR Anthony Knowles/Susan Edwards
A PORCUPINE NAMED FLUFFY Helen Lester/Lynn Munsinger
ALPHABATICS Suse MacDonald
THERE'S SOMETHING SPOOKY IN MY ATTIC Mercer Mayer
ON THE WAY HOME Jill Murphy
HARRY'S NIGHT OUT Abigail Pizer
NOSEY GILBERT Abigail Pizer
HENRIETTA GOOSE Abigail Pizer
THE PIRATE PIG Anne Tyrrell/Cathie Shuttleworth
SIXES AND SEVENS John Yeoman/Quentin Blake
THE BEAR'S WINTER HOUSE John Yeoman/Quentin Blake
THE BEAR'S WATER PICNIC John Yeoman/Quentin Blake

For a complete list of Picturemac titles write to:

Macmillan Children's Books,
18–21 Cavaye Place, London SW10 9PG